D1414293

JONAS **SALK**

Medical Innovator and Polio Vaccine Developer

JONAS **SALK**

Medical Innovator and Polio Vaccine Developer

BY SHEILA LLANAS

CONTENT CONSULTANT
DANIEL J. WILSON
PROFESSOR OF HISTORY
MUHLENBERG COLLEGE

ABDO
Publishing Company

CREDITS

Published by ABDO Publishing Company, PO Box 398166, Minneapolis, MN 55439.
Copyright © 2014 by Abdo Consulting Group, Inc. International copyrights reserved
in all countries. No part of this book may be reproduced in any form without written
permission from the publisher. The Essential Library™ is a trademark and logo of ABDO
Publishing Company.

Printed in the United States of America,
North Mankato, Minnesota
052013
092013

 THIS BOOK CONTAINS AT LEAST 10% RECYCLED MATERIALS.

Editor: Rebecca Felix
Series Designer: Becky Daum

Photo credits: Derek Berwin/Getty Images, cover, 2; Archive Photos/Getty Images, 6;
NYPL/Science Source/Getty Images, 10; AP Images, 17, 21, 36, 40, 64, 75, 78, 80;
Seth Poppel/Yearbook Library, 18, 25; Matty Zimmerman/AP Images, 28; Shutterstock
Images, 34; iStockphoto/Thinkstock, 44; Al Fenn/Time Life Pictures/Getty Images, 48,
60; Alfred Eisenstaedt/Time Life Pictures/Getty Images, 50; Omikron Omikron/Getty
Images, 56; Henry Griffin/AP Images, 58; National Foundation March of Dimes/AP
Images, 68; Preston Stroup/AP Images, 70; George Skadding/Time Life Pictures/Getty
Images, 76; Charles Gorry/AP Images, 87; Jeff Badge/Alamy, 88; Laurent Rebours/AP
Images, 91; Karen Kasmauski/Science Faction/Getty Images, 95

Library of Congress Control Number: 2013932924

Cataloging-in-Publication Data

Llanas, Sheila.
 Jonas Salk : medical innovator and polio vaccine developer / Sheila Llanas.
  p. cm. -- (Essential lives)
 ISBN 978-1-61783-896-5
 Includes bibliographical references and index.
 1. Salk, Jonas, 1914-1995--Health--Juvenile literature. 2. Virologists--United States--
Biography--Juvenile literature. 3. Poliomyelitis vaccine--Juvenile literature. I. Title.
 579.2/092--dc23
 [B]   2013932924

CONTENTS

CHAPTER ONE

ON THE VERGE OF A BREAKTHROUGH

In 1952, Doctor Jonas Salk directed the Virus Research Laboratory at the University of Pittsburgh. In a spacious laboratory located in the lower level of a city hospital, he studied viruses, which are small, infectious agents that cause diseases. Viruses grow in living cells of humans and animals. To study them, Salk needed the most advanced equipment available at the time. He also employed 50 skilled technicians, assistants, and scientists to aid him in his research.

In five years of studying polio, Salk had made some progress. He had also managed to stay out of the public eye. But polio rates were increasing rapidly. Salk's work eventually caught the attention of the public. People were desperate to get rid of poliomyelitis, or polio, a crippling disease caused by an infectious virus that was spreading like wildfire. Word had spread that Salk was toiling away creating a polio vaccine in his laboratory.

Jonas Salk became famous for his work with viruses and vaccines.

POLIO OUTBREAKS

The first major polio outbreak on record struck 44 people in Stockholm, Sweden, in 1887.[3] In 1894, 123 people contracted polio in in Rutland County, Vermont. Of the 123 people, 18 of them died, and 50 were permanently paralyzed.[4] In 1916, polio infected 27,000 and caused 6,000 deaths in the United States.[5] The epidemic occurred primarily in the northeastern United States. The number of polio cases continued to increase in following years. In 1951, polio infected 28,386 people, and in 1952, the number of cases doubled, putting the count up to 57,879.[6] The disease struck children more than adults. It erupted more often in middle or upper class neighborhoods than in poorer communities, and it spread most in hot weather.

Polio attacks the spine and nervous system in a person who has contracted it. This leads to permanent paralysis and possible death. Polio is spread when people eat or drink contaminated substances. The most common source of contamination is sewer water. The summer of 1952 grew to be the worst year on record for polio outbreaks in the United States. That year, 57,879 people in the United States contracted the disease.[1] Most victims were children, many who lost the ability to move leg and arm muscles. Polio killed 3,145 people in 1952 and it gave 21,269 others permanent paralysis.[2] As the polio count rose, people began panicking. The public clamored for information on a possible polio vaccine. Newspapers were eager to report on

Salk's advances. The National Foundation for Infantile Paralysis (NFIP), also called the March of Dimes, was funding Salk's research, in hopes he would make a victorious discovery. The organization donated a lot of money to Salk's laboratory. The nation was anxiously waiting for results, but this did not cause Salk to feel rushed—he continued methodically conducting his lab work. His vaccine was still in the trial phase and needed time to be tested.

Thirty-six-year-old Salk had witnessed the cruelty of polio. He knew the infectious virus struck without warning and advanced quickly. Upon contracting the virus, perfectly healthy children would first feel feverish and weak. Then their arms and legs began to feel rubbery. Many cases of a bad infection saw children rushed to the hospital, including the hospital where Salk worked. In the worst cases of polio, the disease paralyzed the muscles that controlled breathing. Those people could not breathe by themselves. To survive, these patients would have to lie helplessly inside devices called iron lungs. Iron lungs were artificial respirators made from large metal tubes. They made a whirring sound as they helped patients breathe by applying and releasing pressure to the chest, to force breathing.

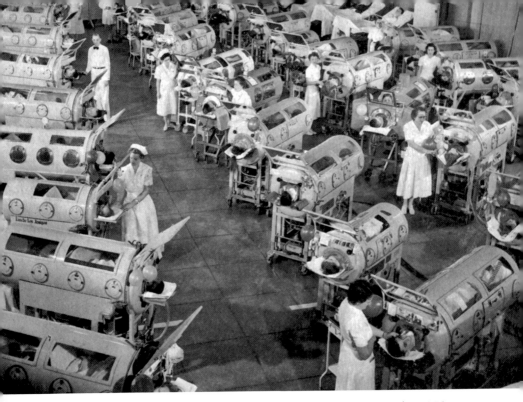
Nurses tending to polio victims in iron lungs in the 1950s

For the general public, and especially for parents who feared their children would catch polio, Salk could not work fast enough.

A Controversial Theory

As people panicked over polio, Salk concentrated on his work. Making a vaccine could be risky. The vaccine itself had to contain a small amount of the virus in order to trigger the immune system. If the process worked, a person's immune system would create antibodies, which are proteins designed to kill the viral cells, thus wiping out the polio. The antibodies created would remain in the body to fight off future exposures. If the vaccine failed, a person could get a case of polio. Salk's job was to create a vaccine too weak to cause the illness but strong enough to trigger the immune system.

To trigger an immune response, researchers believed the polio vaccine had to contain live polio cells. Salk contested that theory and tested a new one. He used killed virus cells—cells that were not living—in his

POLIOMYELITIS: BACKGROUND AND HISTORY

The word *poliomyelitis*, coined in 1878, joins two Greek words. *Poliós* means "grey." *Myelós* means "core" or "marrow." Combined, they refer to the grey matter of the spinal cord. The suffix *–itis* means "inflammation." Poliomyelitis can cause inflammation of the spinal cord's grey matter, injuring the body's nervous system and sometimes causing paralysis or death. There are three types of polio: 1, 2, and 3. Type 1 is the most common, and also the strongest. Each type has many different strains, or subtypes. The paralytic cases, which are the ones associated with the epidemic, represent a minority of the total cases.

Polio is a viral infection. It spreads from person to person through mishandled food, unwashed hands, shared contaminated water, or trace amounts of fecal matter. The virus enters the human body by mouth. It triggers an infection in the small intestine. If antibodies are present in the immune system, the virus will die. If the immune system is not prepared, the infection grows. Immunity to one type of polio does not convey immunity to the other two types. There have been a few people who had polio twice. The majority of polio infections produced an inapparent, or weak, case of the disease, with symptoms resembling a stomach flu, and then the person became immune to that type of polio.

VIROLOGY: STUDYING VIRUSES

Virology is a branch of medicine dealing with viruses and the diseases they cause. As a virologist, Jonas Salk studied the production of antibodies in the immune system. When the body gets a viral infection, blood cells travel to the site. If antibodies for that specific infection exist in the bloodstream, they kill the virus cells. If antibodies do not exist for that specific infection, blood cells called B lymphocytes try to make antibodies. If they succeed, the antibodies stay in the bloodstream to prevent future infections of that virus.

polio vaccine. Salk killed the poliovirus cells using chemicals. He believed using killed cells in his vaccine would be safer, with little to no risk of causing infection. Many medical researchers disagreed with Salk. They worried his killed vaccine would not be potent enough to trigger an immune response and prevent polio.

Salk never intended to create conflict. He simply saw things differently. He trusted his intuition and continued his work, despite criticism. During testing, Salk's vaccine was given to monkeys that did not have polio. The monkeys were able to create antibodies against polio in their blood, and when reexposed to the virus, the monkeys showed no signs of contracting polio. This was encouraging. Salk was ready to take the next step: he needed to test his vaccine on human beings. He hoped it would protect them from polio in the process—not give it to them.

A Human Test

No matter how effective a vaccine proves to be in the laboratory during animal testing, it is medically useless unless it works on people. Testing a new vaccine on people is risky. A trial vaccine created with the intention to protect health can accidentally cause the disease. Because of this risk, the first children Salk chose to test his vaccine already had polio. Using children made testing the polio vaccine additionally risky and controversial. But children were used because many adults had previously had a symptomless or weak case of polio and already had antibodies to the virus. Due to maternal antibodies, infants had some protection against the disease—if infected during this time, they built their own antibodies—but only for a time. Children were the prime victims of the disease, and Salk needed to demonstrate his vaccine could protect children. For the first children Salk tested, who already had

"Why do I see things differently from the way other people see them? Why do I pursue the questions that I pursue, even if others regard them as, as they say, 'controversial?' Which merely means that they have a difference of opinion. They see things differently. I am interested both in nature and in the human side of nature, and how the two can be brought together, and effective in a useful way."[7]
—Jonas Salk

polio, the vaccine would not help them or cure their polio because vaccines only protect healthy people from exposures. So why give the polio-stricken children his vaccine? Because Salk's vaccine would not hurt them either. The polio patients could not get the illness again. However, if the vaccine triggered their immune systems to produce antibodies, it would prove the vaccine could work. Salk would be one step closer to the miracle people were hoping for.

In June 1952, Salk visited the D. T. Watson Home, located near Pittsburgh, Pennsylvania. The institution cared for children who had limbs paralyzed by polio. Salk and a group of nurses took blood samples from a large group of children. First was 16-year-old Bill Kirkpatrick. He had hoped to play football until he got polio. Now he walked with leg braces and crutches. Bill told Salk he would be proud to test the vaccine. He said he would do anything to spare others from getting polio.

In the laboratory, Salk checked the blood samples to determine which of three polio types each child had. On July 2, Salk and his team returned to the D. T. Watson Home. This time, they inoculated the children with Salk's polio vaccine. Once again, Bill bravely went first. The others followed. Salk exposed each child only to the polio type he or she already had. That way, he would not risk giving a child a new case of polio.

Following the test at the D. T. Watson Home, Salk also tested the vaccine on children at the Polk School in Polk, Pennsylvania, an institution for children with mental disabilities, none of whom had previously been exposed to polio. This practice was controversial. Some patients they tested had severe mental disabilities. With their parents' or guardians' permission, Salk tested the vaccine on several children. If any of the patients contracted the disease, Salk's vaccine would be considered a failure. But Salk had confidence. He believed the vaccine would give the patients immunity to the virus.

The D. T. Watson Home children and the Polk School residents went about their daily lives for several

TESTING PATIENTS WITH MENTAL DISABILITIES

In the 1940s and 1950s, some researchers conducted medical studies on disadvantaged populations. Prisoners, terminally ill patients, the poor, people with mental disabilities, and other groups of people were given test drugs and vaccines. Some patients were unable to understand the procedures. Some had not agreed to be tested. In the 1970s and 1980s, the medical community made laws to protect patients' rights. Before receiving any medical treatment, a patient had to give informed consent. It ensured a patient understood and agreed to any medical procedures.

weeks. They could not feel the vaccine at work in their systems. At the end of those two weeks, Salk and the nurses again drew blood from the children at both institutions. Salk felt excited and nervous to discover how children responded to the vaccine. Testing the samples would reveal whether their blood was full of antibodies, and whether any who had not been previously exposed had contracted the disease.

Salk gathered the samples and returned to his lab. One of his assistants, Elsie Ward, lined up test tubes. She began to test for antibodies in the blood cells. First, she did a color test. Into each test tube filled with a blood sample, she mixed poliovirus and a drop of pink dye. The dye was sensitive to acidity levels. If the poliovirus thrived, the weakened blood cells would be low in acid. The test tubes would turn bright pinkish red, a signal of failure. If antibodies were present, and killed the poliovirus, however, the healthy blood cells would have high acid levels, and the dye would turn yellow, signaling success. They had to wait 24 hours to find out.

The next morning, Ward looked at the test tubes and let out a whoop. Salk and other team members came running. All of the test tubes were bright yellow.

Salk enjoyed the exacting work of test studies, which can involve close examination and monitoring of hundreds of test tube samples.

The staff members beamed and cheered. The vaccine had worked. Salk himself merely smiled, keeping calm, which was his typical manner. The vaccine worked on the first batch of testers, but the study was far from over. Salk needed to test the vaccine again, on another test group. This time, the field trial would be larger. In fact, it would be the largest field trial in US history.

CHAPTER
TWO

A DRIVEN STUDENT

Jonas Salk was born on October 28, 1914. His parents, Dora and Daniel, lived in an apartment in Manhattan in New York City, New York. Jonas's mother, Dora Press, immigrated to the United States from Russia by herself when she was 12 years old. In New York City, she found work in a garment factory. Daniel Salk also worked in the clothing industry. He designed lace collars, scarves, and blouses. Daniel had been born in New Jersey. But his family, like Dora, had immigrated to the United States from Russia. Both Daniel's family and Dora had left Russia to escape persecution for being Jewish.

A New York Childhood

When Jonas was two, in 1916, polio erupted in pockets across the United States. In New York City, polio became epidemic, striking more than 9,000 people and killing 2,343 of those afflicted.[1] Health officials imposed quarantines, which meant polio patients were isolated

Jonas as a boy

as much as possible. Posters were stapled to homes where polio hit to warn passersby. The Salks, similar to everyone else, read the warnings and stayed away from those neighborhoods. They avoided the homes of anyone unlucky enough to contract the disease.

As a new mother, Dora fiercely protected her son's health. She learned all she could about polio. At the time, it was called infantile paralysis. Dora did not read English well, so she asked Daniel to read the newspaper aloud to her. The news articles frightened her. They listed the number of polio cases but reported few scientific facts about the disease.

In case the disease spread through germs, Dora kept the family's apartment spotless. She kept Jonas away from other children. She asked Daniel to leave his shoes outside the door when he came home from work. Dora was right to suspect polio was caused by germs. But how did it spread? How could it be prevented? Why did it occur more in hot summer weather? People knew almost nothing about the frightening disease.

Jonas was four on Armistice Day, November 11, 1918. Everyone was celebrating the end of World War I (1914–1918). Even the Salks risked joining the crowds of happy people in Manhattan's streets. Jonas sat on his

The Salks were a part of the massive crowd celebrating Armistice Day in New York City on November 11, 1918.

father's shoulder and watched a parade. He saw soldiers who had just returned from fighting in Europe. Some of them struggled to walk. They used crutches, wore bandages, or had missing limbs. Jonas never forgot the wounded veteran soldiers. Around that same time, Jonas also saw many children using crutches to walk. Even at that young age, he felt concern for people in pain.

At the tail end of the grim years of World War I, another disease, influenza, or flu, surfaced. An estimated 675,000 Americans died of the flu in the 1918–1919 epidemic.[2] The flu also became a military concern. The War Department estimated at least

FRANKLIN D. ROOSEVELT CONTRACTS POLIO

In the summer of 1921, politician Franklin Delano Roosevelt was on vacation with his family on Campobello Island in Canada, off the coast of Maine. On August 10, Roosevelt swam in the Atlantic Ocean and helped fight a forest fire. Later, he felt tired when he sat down to read his mail. When he also felt chilled, he went to bed. When Roosevelt woke up, his knee felt weak. The next day, he could not walk. It appeared an illness had struck him hard and fast. At 39 years old, Roosevelt was diagnosed with polio. It was national news. Roosevelt regained the use of his arms, but he wore braces on his legs and walked with a cane or crutches for the rest of his life.

In 1927, Roosevelt founded the Warm Springs Institute for Rehabilitation, a center to help polio victims in Georgia. Roosevelt was elected president of the United States in 1932, and began his role the next year. He would be president until his death in 1945. In 1938, he founded the National Foundation for Infantile Paralysis (NFIP). The organization, now known as the March of Dimes, raised money to fund polio research. The NFIP also funded the education of nurses and physical therapists in the treating of polio patients, care for polio patients, and the purchase of devices such as wheelchairs. After Roosevelt died, some researchers doubted his polio diagnosis, thinking he may have contracted a rare disorder called Guillain-Barré Syndrome instead.

26 percent of army personnel contracted influenza.[3] After the terrible influenza epidemic, fears of polio soon returned.

When Jonas was nearly seven years old, an event happened that would help determine his future work. In August 1921, well-known New York politician Franklin Delano Roosevelt was diagnosed with polio. The *New York Times* broke the news on September 16, 1921. The news shocked and saddened many, including the Salks. Dora and Daniel had no idea at the time their son would one day work to prevent both influenza and polio.

An Advanced Student

Jonas was five when his brother Herman was born, and 12 when his brother Lee was born. With three boys to raise, the Salks moved to the more affordable Brooklyn borough of New York City. Jonas was a quiet, sensitive young person. He was the kind of person who observed the world around him. He thought deeply about what he saw. He could imagine himself in the position of other people or objects. He could feel the suffering of others. These thought patterns would later aid him in his career as a scientist.

"I was not a great reader. I spent a good deal of time thinking, as I still do, about what went on in my life, my own observations and reflections. I did read what was part of schooling, but I was not an avid reader. There are a few significant books that I recall: Michael Hunter's *Life of Louis Pasteur*. I remember reading, as an adolescent, a book called *The Island Within* by Ludwig Lewisohn. The idea of the 'island within' gives you the sense of the resonance that this had for me, because of my sense of myself, and the dialogues that I had with myself."[4]

— *Jonas Salk*

Due to his intelligence, Jonas skipped several grades and was able to begin high school at the young age of 12. He attended Townsend Harris High School for the humanities, a top school for advanced students located in New York City. Students at Townsend had to work hard, learning four years worth of material in only three years. Jonas had no trouble with this. He excelled in school and was good at studying.

Jonas's scholarly inclinations were not inherited. His parents never received any formal education and he did not have any other role models who had been to school. But his parents supported him and urged him to succeed. Jonas often discussed school matters with his parents, as well as his goals for the future. At the time, Jonas had not yet considered studying science, and Townsend was a school that emphasized history and literature. Jonas did take physics

Jonas's senior high school portrait

there, which was the only science class offered, but he planned to study law in the future. His mother asked Jonas how he could win a court case if he could not even win an argument with her. Jonas then declared he

THE CITY COLLEGE OF NEW YORK

The City College of New York was founded in 1847. By the time Jonas enrolled in 1931, more and more students there came from Jewish families. At the time, many other schools discriminated against Jewish students. Similar to Jonas, their parents had escaped persecution and discrimination in Eastern and Central Europe for being Jewish. These young people were first-generation Americans. They were often the first in their families to attend college. Many lived in New York's poor neighborhoods. In a time when the Great Depression imposed economic hardships, City College represented a chance to achieve higher goals.

was not going to be a lawyer: he wanted to be a congressman instead. He graduated high school with top grades when he was 15 years old. Though his parents were not rich, they assured Jonas he would be able to attend college.

Choices in College

In 1929, at 15 years old, Jonas entered the City College of New York. He was the first person in his family to go to college. He earned scholarships to pay part of the tuition, and his parents scraped together the rest of the money. Jonas could pay them back, they said, by getting a good education. He declared pre-law as his major. However, the City College encouraged students to explore all areas. They required students to take classes outside of their main interest. In his first year, Jonas signed up for chemistry. The class thrilled him, opening his eyes to a new world and awakening a deep interest within him.

Jonas changed his mind about going into politics. He decided to study laws of science, not society. He later said, "I found myself interested now in the laws of nature, as distinct from the laws the people make."[5] Jonas began thinking about medicine. But he was not necessarily interested in treating patients. Rather, he wanted to use science to study medicine. By the time Jonas earned his undergraduate degree in 1934, his goal was to work as a medical researcher.

CHAPTER
THREE

MEDICAL SCHOOL

After earning his degree at the City College of New York, Salk decided to further his education. When Salk applied to medical school, he was prepared for rejection. If that happened, he decided he would work instead toward a graduate degree in endocrinology, which is a branch of biology. Salk never had to use his back-up plan. In the fall of 1934, he entered the New York University School of Medicine. The campus was close to the home where Salk lived with his parents, stacking textbooks in his bedroom. At 19, he was younger than his classmates, and he was still a quiet person who preferred studying to socializing. Studying science meant memorizing a lot of factual information. But Salk did not blindly accept facts. He thought deeply about what he learned. He questioned proven theories. He puzzled over information that was presented as true.

In one class, Salk learned about vaccines and viruses. The principles were simple: to become immune, or

Later in life, Salk received honors from his first alma mater, the City College of New York, for his work on the polio vaccine.

protected, from a disease, a person had to be exposed to a vaccine. A vaccine was made with viral cells that have been reduced in force. Vaccines are capable of provoking the body's creation of antibodies, or proteins that kill viruses. Antibodies kill the virus before it can cause the disease. Antibodies also allow the body to fight off a later infection of the virus. Medically, illnesses related to viruses had to be treated differently from bacterial illnesses. Bacteria, which are one-celled organisms lacking a nucleus, reproduce rapidly, are found everywhere on earth, and serve many functions. Bacteria do not need living tissue to grow, as viruses do. Bacterial vaccines, Salk's professor explained, could be made of inactivated, or killed, bacteria. Killed vaccines worked only on bacterial diseases. The professor stressed the point. Bacterial vaccines contained inactivated or killed bacteria. Viral vaccines contained active virus. Viral vaccines should be too weak to cause infection, but sometimes the weak virus cells mutated back to dangerous levels. The living vaccine could then cause a full-blown viral illness. Living viral vaccines were not as safe as killed bacterial vaccines. With those remarks, the professor dismissed the class.

Salk puzzled over these ideas. Something seemed wrong to him. He did not yet know what. He questioned the principles. Why did viral vaccines have to be made from active virus cells? Was there a way to make a safe killed viral vaccine? Salk stayed after class to talk with his professor. He wanted to learn more and explore the ideas. His professor dismissed Salk's questions. He said

VIRUSES

In 1898, Dutch botanist Martinus Beijerinck studied sickly tobacco plants. He strained plant liquid to separate bacteria. Instead, another substance slipped through his filter. It was not bacteria. Rubbing it on healthy leaves made them sick. This told him the cells were living and could reproduce. Beijerinck named the contagious substance *virus*, the Latin word for poison.

Beijerinck's discovery was amazing, considering he could not see the virus. A microscope strong enough to see viral cells had not been invented yet. Similar to bacteria, viruses are invisible to the naked eye. Viruses are even smaller than bacteria. Bacterial cells are complex enough to grow outside of living tissue. Viral cells are too simple. They cannot reproduce on their own. Viruses need a host, meaning they grow only in other living cells.

Bacterial illnesses can be treated with antibiotics. Examples are strep throat, cholera, and tuberculosis. Viral illnesses cannot be treated with antibiotics. To prevent viruses, a vaccine must be given before exposure. Chickenpox, influenza, shingles, herpes, HIV, and the common cold are all examples of human viral diseases. Many of these viral illnesses do not yet have vaccines.

the proven theory was true and that was all there was to it. Viral vaccines helped thousands of people. They were worth the risk of a few people getting sick.

The professor's answers did not satisfy Salk. He left the classroom, but he could not stop thinking about it. There must be a way to make a safer viral vaccine. But how? He did not know the answer, but he thought about the question all the time.

A Research Assistant

Salk was not a typical medical student—he had no interest in becoming a doctor. In that case, it might have been easier for Salk to earn a PhD in science rather than medicine. But Salk had a specific reason for studying medicine: he wanted to conduct medical research. A chemistry professor, Doctor R. Keith Cannan, noticed Salk's unique position. The professor offered Salk the opportunity to work in his lab as a research assistant. If Salk accepted the offer, he would take one year away from medical school. He would therefore graduate one year later than his classmates. He would receive no credit toward his degree while he assisted in Cannan's lab, and the pay was low. Explaining all this to Salk, Cannan told the student to think about the decision.

"At one point at the end of my first year of medical school, I received an opportunity to spend a year in research and teaching in biochemistry, which I did. And at the end of that year, I was told that I could, if I wished, switch and get a PhD in biochemistry but my preference was to stay with medicine. And, I believe that this is all linked to my original ambition, or desire, which was to be of some help to humankind, so to speak, in a larger sense than just on a one-to-one basis."[1]
—Jonas Salk

Salk accepted the job immediately. Laboratory research was his main interest. Hands-on experience as a medical researcher would be invaluable. Salk spent the academic year of 1935–1936 in Cannan's biochemistry lab. Cannan worked on an infectious illness caused by streptococcus bacteria, or strep. Symptoms of strep began with sore throat and fever. From there, the illness

could remain mild, or it could turn severe. Cannan studied the strep bacteria to see if he could make an inactive, or killed, vaccine.

To study bacteria, the lab needed large amounts of it. Salk's task was to grow strep in a culture, or liquid mix. The next step was to pour the mix into a centrifuge, a machine that rotated with so much force the contents separated. While Salk spun the mix, the strep bacteria separated from the culture, and he was able to extract pure bacteria from the bottom of the container. The machine allowed Salk to spin only a small amount of mix at a time. This led Salk to make a choice. He could continue doing the tedious task over and over again. Or, he realized, he could conduct an experiment of his own and find a faster method of separating the bacteria. Salk decided he wanted a faster method.

He wondered if freezing the mix would force it to separate faster. He added calcium phosphate, a chemical used to speed the freezing process, to ice. He placed a sealed can of strep culture safely inside a larger container filled with his mix of ice and calcium phosphate. He tried to freeze the strep solution several times. Each time, he failed to separate bacteria. Then, he accidentally spilled calcium phosphate directly into the container. When he drained the liquid, he found pure bacterial germ cells!

Salk ran the test again and again. He got the same successful results every time. He could now separate bacterial cells quickly without a centrifuge. He learned firsthand that, in scientific experiments, there are no failures. Research, he saw, is always a process of learning. Salk's results impressed Cannan. Salk wrote an article and published his scientific discovery. As a first-year medical student, Salk had already taken big steps toward his career.

Thomas Francis, *left*, met Salk, *right*, while Salk was in college. Francis became an important mentor and colleague to Salk throughout his career.

Finishing Medical School

Salk completed two more years of medical school. With one more year to go, he spent the summer of 1938 in Woods Hole, Massachusetts, working as a lab technician. While there, Salk met Donna Lindsay, a young woman who was there on vacation. She had a psychology degree from Smith College in Northampton, Massachusetts, and studied at the New York School of Social Work. Salk and Donna had many values in common. They both chose fields of work that helped humanity. Donna was smart, compassionate, and easy to talk to. Salk could be himself around her. They began dating.

That fall, during his final year of medical school, Salk met another person who became influential in his life. Doctor Thomas Francis, a virologist and microbiologist, studied influenza in Manhattan at the New York University School of Medicine. It was the viral disease that caused the epidemic of 1918–1919. Francis wanted to create an inactive, or killed, flu vaccine. Salk, keenly interested in this topic, volunteered to work in Francis's lab. This time, Salk grew virus cells, not bacteria. His task while assisting Francis was to kill the flu virus

ROCKEFELLER INSTITUTE FOR MEDICAL RESEARCH

As a research assistant, Salk often visited the Rockefeller Institute for Medical Research. The institute was founded in June 1901, by American entrepreneur and industrialist John D. Rockefeller Sr. Rockefeller was also the founder of the successful, dominant force in the oil industry, Standard Oil Company. The Rockefeller Institute for Medical Research was the first biomedical institute in the United States. People called it simply the Rockefeller Institute. The institute existed for the study of infectious diseases using chemistry, physics, microbiology, and other sciences. At the time, contagious illnesses such as tuberculosis, diphtheria, typhoid fever, and polio were the greatest threats to human health.

with ultraviolet radiation. Fortunately, the Rockefeller Institute, the only lab that had the needed equipment, was close by. Salk carried the virus from Twenty-Fourth Street north to Sixty-Sixth Street. There, he would zap the virus cells with radiation. Then he would hurry back to campus where Francis would study the results. Salk learned a lot during his time assisting in labs. Then he refocused on completing his coursework.

Salk graduated from medical school on June 8, 1939. Officially a doctor, he added the title to his name. The day after he received his diploma, on June 9, he and Donna married. Salk made another name change that day, this one to please his new father-in-law. Salk's parents never gave him a middle name. To Donna's father, Salk's full name seemed incomplete without a middle name. Salk chose the name Edward, after a favorite British royal, and began using the name Doctor Jonas E. Salk.

After graduating, Salk next had to complete a two-year internship as part of his degree. This required stage would give him hands-on training as a doctor. He applied to intern at Mount Sinai Hospital in Manhattan. Salk was one of 12 interns chosen from approximately 250 other top applicants.[2] In March 1940, Salk began caring for patients and attending lectures as part of his internship. Salk's patients found him gentle and compassionate. He excelled in diagnosing illnesses. But Salk still spent every spare moment in the research laboratory. His fascination for viruses and vaccines continued growing.

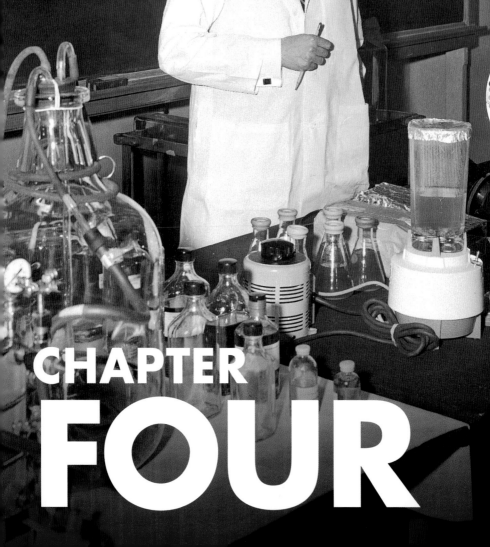

CHAPTER
FOUR

BUDDING VIROLOGIST

When Salk entered virology, the field was still new. Even the word *virus* had only been coined 40 years earlier. Virus cells cannot be seen with a regular microscope. They thrive in the human body, but were hard to grow in the lab. Salk had taken on quite a challenge.

By 1938, two events had happened that aided Salk's research in different ways. One was the invention of the electron microscope the year before. It could magnify an object 7,000 times, allowing researchers to see and learn more about both bacteria and viruses.[1]

The other event was the founding of nonprofit organization the NFIP in 1938. Founded by President Roosevelt, the organization became known as the March of Dimes after the organization asked kids to donate a dime each to fight polio. Its mission was to study polio, which Roosevelt had survived years earlier.

The invention of several scientific technologies aided Salk in his research.

Local chapters formed to advertise for the NFIP, raise awareness of polio, and collect donations. The NFIP used the money to fund polio research as well as rehabilitation of people stricken with the disease.

Helping the Army

In 1942, Salk completed his internship at Mount Sinai Hospital. It was time for him to decide what his next step would be. Francis had become head of the Department of Epidemiology at the University of Michigan, and he offered Salk a job in his lab. During this time, however, beginning in 1941, the United States fought in World War II (1939–1945). Salk felt he had a duty to serve in the war. He responded to Francis's offer by letter, explaining he planned to enlist and become a military doctor. Francis quickly wrote back. Soldiers were dying from raging influenza epidemics. The disease had become a military issue. And Francis was the director of the Commission on Influenza for the army— the army had asked him to create a safe influenza vaccine. Therefore, if Salk worked for Francis, he would also be working for and serving the army. He could help thousands of soldiers rather than just a few.

Salk was convinced. At 27 years old, he agreed to join a team of medical specialists in Francis's lab. In 1942, he and Donna packed up their home in New York and moved west to Ann Arbor, Michigan. Apartments near campus were too pricey for Salk's salary of $2,100 a year, so the Salks rented the second floor of a farmhouse outside of town.[2] The landlords lived downstairs. They cooked on a wood-burning stove that also heated their rooms. In rain and snow, the dirt roads washed out, but Salk loved living in the country. He enjoyed gardening, yard work, and chopping wood. Nature seemed like a larger version of the microscopic world he studied in his laboratory.

UNIVERSITY OF MICHIGAN SCHOOL OF PUBLIC HEALTH

The School of Public Health at the University of Michigan was founded in 1941. That year, the school invited Francis to build a virus lab and start the Department of Epidemiology. The department's mission was to study diseases in order to promote health in the United States and worldwide. Salk was one of the first researchers Francis invited to assist him.

Since being established, the University of Michigan School of Public Health has risen to become one of the most respected and top-ranked health schools in the country. As of 2013, the Department of Health Management and Policy had ranked it the top health-care program in the United States every year since 1993.

Salk would spend five years researching at the University of Michigan in Ann Arbor.

A Virologist in the Making

At his new job on campus, Salk taught classes in epidemiology in addition to conducting research in the lab. Aiding Francis in his work on a flu vaccine, Salk's job, once again, was to isolate the virus, as he had done as a research assistant for Cannan years before. Salk tried separating the cells using calcium phosphate, as he had in Cannan's lab. But the process did not produce enough virus cells. It did not work as well as it did with bacteria. Salk decided that rather than grow viruses in culture, he needed a new method. It was the kind of puzzle he loved to solve. Viruses always need host cells. Scientists had already proven viruses grown in blood cells are easy to remove. Salk decided to grow the flu virus in chicken eggs. Kept at the right temperatures, and put through an exact series of warmings, washings, and salt treatments, the virus could easily be separated. After several trials, Salk soon had a concentrated supply of the virus. He wrote another article on his discovery, this time for *Science* magazine. In the list of authors for the piece, Francis's name was credited before Salk's. This was a common practice. Although Salk had done the work, it was Francis's lab, and researchers in a lab worked as a team. The lab director and all other lab assistants received credit for one researcher's work.

A short time later, Salk wrote a follow-up article. This time, he asked Francis if his name could go first in the publication. Francis hesitated. In the world of science, researchers typically shared

SALK'S *SCIENCE* MAGAZINE ARTICLES

Science magazine was founded in 1880 with $10,000 donated by US inventor Thomas Edison.[3] From 1942 until 1993, Salk published at least eight articles in the journal. The first was published on November 27, 1942. Its title was "A Simplified Procedure for the Concentration and Purification of Influenza Virus," by Thomas Francis Jr. and Jonas E. Salk.

credit. Individuals did not seek their own credit. But Francis knew his former student was an independent thinker and a leader. He agreed to let Salk's name be listed first.

Testing the Flu Vaccine

Salk still often thought about the question he had pondered as a first year medical student. Could he destroy a virus and make a safe vaccine? Everyone he asked told him it would not work. It had never been done before. It was commonly believed viral vaccines worked only with living virus cells. But live vaccines could cause a person to become sick, and Salk did not want a single person to become sick using vaccines. He decided to begin researching this subject. He knew he might not get the results he wanted but was willing to fail on the chance that he might succeed.

> "Risks, I like to say, always pay off. You learn what to do or what not to do."[4]
> —Jonas Salk

Salk shared his aspiration with Francis, and the two created a flu vaccine from killed virus cells and tested it on mice. It was a great success. None of the mice became sick from the vaccine. That meant the killed virus vaccine worked, and it was then ready for human testing. Ideally, the killed virus would act similarly in humans and not cause anyone to get sick. In September 1943, Salk set up a clinic in an empty classroom at a Michigan army camp. He injected 20 volunteer soldiers with the test flu vaccine.[5] After three days, he checked their blood samples under the microscope. The results were amazing: each man's immune system had produced antibodies.

The next step was to test whether the volunteers were actually immune to the flu. This step was risky, as Salk did not want to infect his patients if the vaccine had not worked. Salk swabbed flu germs right into the soldiers' noses and throats. Then he quarantined them, isolating them from others to prevent a possible flu outbreak. Three days later, he tested their blood and found strong antibodies. To his relief, all 20 volunteers were strong and healthy. They had immunity from the virus, at least for a time. Salk and Francis had successfully created a killed-virus vaccine. Their invention and discovery were groundbreaking.

Salk traveled to more army bases. In all, he tested the vaccine on approximately 12,000 army personnel.[6] Next, the Commission on Influenza conducted a larger

Their successful collaboration to create the killed virus vaccine for the flu in 1943 would not be the last time Francis, *left*, and Salk, *right*, worked together.

vaccine trial. Late in 1943, Salk and Francis inoculated 25,000 college students.[7] But not all received the vaccine. Half the students received the vaccine, and the other half received a placebo made of saline. Those who received the vaccine did not come down with the flu during the season it was most common. Many with the placebo did. As results came in, it became clear: the vaccine worked to prevent the flu. Everyone in the lab celebrated. Francis was credited with the discovery of the breakthrough vaccine, and he went on to lead larger field trials. He also discovered that, because flu strains change every year, the vaccine must be adjusted annually. The flu vaccine was soon put into widespread use.

Salk's contribution to the flu vaccine was over. Salk and his wife also celebrated the birth of their first son, Peter, in January 1944. Two years later, the Salks were expecting another baby. They had outgrown the upstairs apartment in the old farmhouse. The Salks rented a larger home in time for their son Darrell to be born in March 1947. Their third son, Jonathan, was born in 1950.

During his years in Francis's lab, Salk had moved up from research fellow to associate professor. He had aided in important discoveries to the field that included treatment of influenza, pneumonia, and other infections. In that time, Salk had learned a lot from his mentor Francis. But he felt it was time to move on, and he decided to look for a new job. What Salk really wanted was to direct his own laboratory. Francis was not surprised. He knew his student was ready.

CHAPTER
FIVE

A LAB OF HIS OWN

In May 1947, Salk applied to direct a lab in California. He did not get the job. But Salk had become known in the field. And it seemed people at the University of Pittsburgh had heard Salk was job hunting. The medical school dean offered Salk a position directing their virus laboratory. When Salk visited the campus, he found a cramped basement lab. It was not nearly as glamorous or attractive as the California lab where he had applied. The Pittsburgh medical school promised more space and funding. They also offered Salk the opportunity to research a topic of his choice. Some people felt taking the job at Pittsburgh would be a mistake. But Salk saw it as an opportunity. He accepted the position.

Salk was director of a dark laboratory in the basement of a city hospital. He had poor equipment, a small staff, and almost no money. He spent his first year applying for grants. He hired a few research assistants. Most important, he decided on a field of his choice. Already having worked with strep and influenza,

Salk's first lab in Pittsburgh was cramped and empty, but he was soon granted an expansion stocked with medical research technology.

Salk wanted a new challenge. He decided to focus his research on polio.

Studying Polio

Polio intrigued Salk. In 1947, much about the disease was still a mystery. Good hygiene did not stop it. Not every carrier contracted it. No blood test could detect

POLIO ON THE RISE

Cases of polio rose dramatically after 1900. The disease often struck residents of the cleanest homes. This baffled people. How could cleanliness invite infection? It turned out that modern sanitation actually helped spread polio by introducing people to it later in life. Prior to the late 1880s, people lived closer to the earth. They did not have plumbing and they did not clean every surface with cleansers and disinfectants. People worked with the soil to grow their own food. They lived close to chickens, pigs, cows, and horses. In these agrarian environments, babies were often exposed to tiny amounts of the poliovirus, among other things. Babies' immune systems are strong and growing. Babies also are somewhat protected by maternal antibodies in the first months of life as they build their own antibody response. As babies are busily developing, their immune systems easily make antibodies. Therefore, babies who were exposed early created a natural defense and often grew up protected from polio. In cleaner modern environments, infants were not exposed to polio. By the time they were older, their bodies did not make antibodies as easily. Those who were not exposed to polio as babies were at a greater risk of getting infected with polio and becoming paralyzed. Without early exposure, their bodies did not naturally develop immunity. As Salk said, "As hygienic conditions improved, the virus spread in the population in a different way than it did when hygienic conditions were poor."[1]

it before it grew deadly. Polio cells quickly grew in the human body, but they were hard to grow in a lab. Polio presented the kind of challenge Salk enjoyed working on. He studied the tiny cells of the disease in the quiet privacy of his own laboratory. Before long, Salk's choice of study attracted attention.

In December 1947, Salk received a visit from the director of research of the NFIP, Harry Weaver. Weaver saw Salk's empty lab and smiled. He smiled because he saw an opportunity. Weaver wanted to fund a few labs to study polio. The NFIP would grant the university that ran the lab a couple hundred thousand dollars a year to do so. Salk could build a decent laboratory with quality equipment. There was, however, one condition. Salk first had to type polio. By 1949, researchers had identified three classes of poliovirus: types 1, 2, and 3. But no one had identified the various strains in each type. There might be hundreds. To receive the NFIP grant, Salk would have to identify every strain. The typing project could take years, requiring the scientist behind it to have great patience.

Other scientists might turn down such long, tedious work. But Salk characteristically made a fast decision. He felt as though he was in the right place at the right time. Salk knew any chance he had at making a polio vaccine would depend on the typing results. He shook hands with Weaver and accepted the offer.

Salk began building a dream laboratory. With the NFIP support, it was easy to get access to more space. The rooms on either side of his basement lab were cleared for his use. Salk bought new equipment and hired a staff of assistant researchers. He turned his hospital facility into a modern virology laboratory.

Typing Polio

By 1949, Salk's laboratory took up two floors and work on typing polio was underway. Salk and his team gathered throat cultures and stool samples from polio victims across the country. They tested and catalogued these human samples. They also injected monkeys with strains of polio. Then they tested the animal tissue to identify the type of polio. One area in the lab housed all the monkeys—close to 1,800—used for testing.[2] As he worked, Salk set about finding faster, more efficient methods of typing the polio strains. Even so, he and his staff worked 12 hours a day, six or seven days a week, from 1949 to 1952.

In the summer of 1949, the national toll of polio cases reached 42,033.[3] Salk sometimes visited the polio wards that were located on the floors above his lab at the hospital. Many children in the wards were treated for paralysis. Some of them needed iron lungs to breathe. Seeing these children reminded Salk why he was working so hard.

The purpose of Salk's typing was to create a vaccine that could treat all three types of polio. In 1950, although his typing was not yet complete, Salk was convinced he could develop a killed polio vaccine and wanted to try. Because the NFIP funded his lab, Salk had to ask them for permission. In the spring of that year, Salk requested approval to work on a polio vaccine. The NFIP told him to complete the typing project first.

Salk completed the typing project in 1951. He and his team discovered 196 strains. They all fit into the three types. Type I led to 82 percent of all paralytic

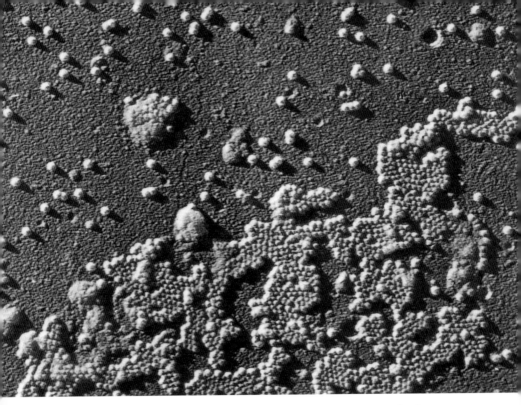

A microscopic view of poliovirus

polio cases, type 2 was responsible for approximately
10 percent, and type 3 for 8 percent.[4]

In the summer of 1951, Salk traveled on an
ocean liner to Copenhagen, Denmark, to attend an
international polio conference. He presented his findings
on typing polio at the conference. Albert Sabin, a
US scientist who was working to make a live polio
vaccine, also attended the conference. As a result of the
information shared at the conference, the NFIP finally
approved the pursuit of a vaccine, funding both Salk and
Sabin's ventures.

Live Vaccine versus Killed Vaccine

Salk could not have done his own work without earlier scientific discoveries. He did not agree with all the current theories, however. He had ideas of his own. One of his ideas, in particular, caused conflict in the research community. Many researchers, including Sabin, advocated making a living polio vaccine. Antibodies built first in the stomach, then the blood. Therefore, these scientists reasoned, people could be injected with active poliovirus cells, or the live vaccine could be taken orally. This way, the vaccine would enter a person's system exactly as the poliovirus would itself. The living vaccine would hopefully shock the immune system into building antibodies, right where the vaccine had entered. If the vaccine did not incite this reaction, however, a case of full-blown polio would result. It was a high-risk equation, which Salk wanted to avoid.

Salk believed a killed virus vaccine would be safer. He added the chemical formaldehyde to the mix to kill

LIVE VIRUS VACCINE TRIAL

In 1934 and 1935, public health researchers in Philadelphia tested a live virus polio vaccine. Ten thousand healthy people were inoculated. Tragically, the vaccine itself caused ten cases of paralysis and five deaths.[5]

Salk, *left*, and Sabin, *right*, were scientific opponents, each advocating for their own version of polio vaccine.

the virus cells. The killed virus would still be strong enough to trigger the immune system, but if the virus in the vaccine was all killed, one could not contract polio. Inoculating patients with the killed virus vaccine was not as simple as with a live virus vaccine, however. The killed virus vaccine had to be given as a series of three injections. Most people dislike receiving shots, especially more than one. Sabin and many other polio researchers at the time were convinced that an attenuated, or weakened, active vaccine provided a stronger antibody response since it mimicked wild polio, or polio that is caught naturally, not through a vaccine. Many also thought the protection from an active virus would last longer than from a killed virus vaccine. Because of these reasons, Salk was often criticized for his theories about developing a killed vaccine.

Although Salk and Sabin worked together on committees and met at conferences, Sabin became one of Salk's biggest opponents. Both scientists treated each other civilly even as they firmly stated their different points of view, however. Salk later said he learned "not only about the human side of nature, but about the human side of science" from the two's opposition.[6]

As a medical scientist, Salk enjoyed exploring unique, creative approaches to human ailments. He was willing to experiment, even if it meant going against mainstream thinking. Salk also did not mind disagreements. Due to his success with a killed influenza virus vaccine, he had confidence in his idea for a poliovirus vaccine. However, he needed time to work on it privately, without hearing opposition from the science community. Salk knew there was no way everyone would agree with him, so his goal became to present proven findings backing his theory.

CHAPTER SIX

TESTING THE VACCINE

Salk faced the same challenge with poliovirus as he had with strep and flu. He needed to gather large quantities of the virus. In the past, Salk had exposed monkeys to poliovirus to create the amount of virus needed. When the monkeys contracted the disease, Salk would harvest the virus cells. In 1949, his method changed when three Harvard University researchers discovered a method for growing virus in non-nerve tissue. This breakthrough gave researchers a safe, efficient method to grow the virus. Salk no longer had to inject laboratory monkeys with poliovirus but instead could grow it in monkey kidney cells in a culture.

Once he had a supply of virus cells, Salk inactivated them with the chemical formaldehyde, creating an early form of his vaccine. To test it, Salk still used monkeys. He inoculated the animals with the vaccine. Within three weeks, he checked the monkeys' blood.

One of Salk's associates inoculates a monkey with the polio vaccine.

Salk found weak polio antibodies in the animals' blood. The antibodies would need to be stronger to make the animals immune to the disease. To achieve this, Salk tried mixing the polio vaccine with mineral oil. The oil would help the vaccine stay in the body longer, thus allowing more time for stronger antibodies to develop. It worked—the monkeys created stronger antibodies. The next step in Salk's test was to prove the monkeys could ward off polio. When Salk exposed the monkeys

GROWING POLIOVIRUS

In 1949, Harvard researchers John R. Enders, Thomas H. Weller, and Frederick C. Robbins discovered how to grow poliovirus outside of living tissue and how to grow it in non-nerve tissues, such as kidney tissue. Their discovery was a milestone in virology. Not only was their method of growing viruses easier and less costly, but it spared the lives of many animals. Their research was essential to the development of both the Salk and Sabin vaccines. Without the ability to grow large amounts of the virus safely, there was no way to create the large number of vaccination doses needed to immunize all children. In 1954, the three Harvard researchers won the Nobel Prize in Physiology or Medicine. In their Nobel Prize lecture, they credited researchers whose earlier work supported theirs: "The results of our research are not alone the product of our triple thought and effort. As nearly always in the undertaking of science many others who have worked with us have contributed of their minds and labor. And so we would think of them as here with us now, sharing in these great happenings."[1]

to polio, not a single monkey got sick. The vaccine successfully prevented polio in animals. It was time to see if it worked in people.

The First Human Tests

In 1952, Salk inoculated healthy children at the Polk School and infected children with his polio vaccine at the D. T. Watson Home. Results were excellent. The children grew strong antibodies in their blood. But Salk stopped the test there and did not expose children to the live poliovirus. Even though he was confident the children were immune, Salk did not want to risk infecting the children who had not already been sick. Instead, he continued to refine his vaccine. Every step forward led to new questions. Salk had to determine the vaccine's dose, as well as how much time to allow between the three shots. Every detail went into making a vaccine just strong enough to trigger a human body to create antibodies—no more, no less. Salk, confident in his vaccine, also injected himself and everyone in his lab. Next, he injected his wife, Donna, and their three sons, Peter, Darrell, and Jonathan.

Salk inoculated himself, his wife, and his three sons with his polio vaccine before conducting a widespread trial.

Making a Public Statement

Typically, a researcher might spend between 10 to 20 years working on a vaccine. Salk had worked on polio for only four years, but he already seemed close to a breakthrough. The nation waited impatiently. Although early results appeared promising, Salk could not risk rushing. As a researcher, he was ready to inform the scientific community of the status of his work, which was standard procedure. He wrote an article for the *Journal of the American Medical Association*. Its title alone was a mouthful: "Studies in Human Subjects on Active

Immunization Against Poliomyelitis: A Preliminary Report of Experiments in Progress." In the article, Salk details his research, charts his findings, and makes one clear point: the vaccine was not ready for widespread use.

Two weeks before Salk's article appeared, the *New York Post* scooped the news. They printed a story with a bold headline, "New Polio Vaccine! Big Hopes Seen!"[2] Salk, rattled, found himself in the public eye. The news story made him look greedy for credit. Worse yet, the sensational story made a claim Salk could not guarantee.

Salk set aside his desire for privacy. The American public needed to know the truth about the polio vaccine, and they needed to hear it directly from him. On March 26, 1953, Salk sat in a booth in a CBS studio in New York City. He spoke into a microphone for 15 minutes in a radio broadcast called "The Scientist Speaks for Himself." In the interview, Salk told listeners he was testing a polio vaccine, but his studies were still incomplete. "Although progress has been more rapid than we had any right to expect," he said, "there will be no vaccine available for widespread use for the next polio season."[3]

The American people were dismayed. They felt results were coming too slowly. Meanwhile, children across the nation continued contracting polio.

Polio Pioneers: The Field Trial Begins

Salk had expanded his vaccine trial when he tested his own children. He vaccinated other children in the Pittsburgh area. The numbers grew to 600.[4] Next, he successfully inoculated more than 4,000 Pittsburgh schoolchildren.[5] In November 1953, the NFIP asked Francis to oversee the field trial of Salk's vaccine. The national field trial took five months to plan, and it was approved on April 25, 1954. It would be the largest trial of an experimental vaccine that was ever attempted. This was partly due to polio being a relatively rare disease. Large numbers of trial patients were needed in order to get statistically significant results.

But Salk encountered a problem. His laboratory was only able to make a small amount of vaccine, which would not be enough to mass-produce it. To create large enough quantities, the NFIP hired several drug companies to make Salk's vaccine on a large scale. Salk tracked the safety of his vaccine as it was created, but he was not given a hands-on role in the field trials. Both Salk and the NFIP were kept out of the trial to avoid any appearance of bias that could taint the results. By funding the vaccine's development, the NFIP had done its part. By inventing the vaccine, Salk had already done his part. As the project expanded, more people became involved, and Salk had little control over the process.

The NFIP funded the trial, raising money from millions of small donations. Many ordinary citizens helped pay for the study through these donations. They also volunteered their time. Approximately 300,000 people—schoolteachers, parents, nurses, and doctors— offered to help however they could with the trial.[8] Many organized immunizations in their local areas.

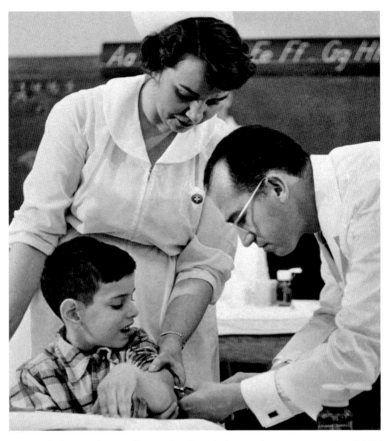

Salk inoculates a boy in Pittsburgh during the vaccine trial in 1954.

The children who were to be involved were
prepared for testing. Many parents were desperate
to protect their children from polio, and they were
willing to try anything. In 44 states, close to
1.8 million schoolchildren were involved in the trial.[9]
They were called Polio Pioneers. Of them, 400,000
were inoculated with the vaccine, and the rest were

either given a placebo or acted as a control group.[10] The field trial was done to determine whether those inoculated had a lower rate of polio in the 1954 polio season than those who received the placebo or those who were merely watched to see if they got polio. No children involved in the trial were injected with active poliovirus. By the time it was finished, Salk's polio vaccine test was the largest field trial ever conducted. It is still a landmark in the history of medicine in the United States. No medical study before or since has equaled in number Salk's vaccine field trial. Families and doctors waited anxiously for the results. On his way to work one morning, Salk passed a gift shop. On the magazine rack, to his surprise, he saw his own face on the cover of *Time* magazine, the issue dated March 29, 1954. "Polio Fighter Salk," the cover caption read. "Is this the year?"[11]

MEDIA COVERAGE OF POLIO VACCINE

The media was eager to report on Salk's progress and often wrote attention-grabbing headlines speculating on his work. On March 12, 1954, a front-page article in the *New York Times* claimed that, "within the next three to five years polio, crippler of young and old alike, will join diphtheria, smallpox, typhoid and other formerly dreaded infectious diseases as plagues finally tamed and conquered by man."[12]

Just weeks later, on March 29, a *Time* magazine issue with his portrait on the cover was released.

CHAPTER
SEVEN

BREAKING NEWS

I t took one year to tally the results of the massive field trial of Salk's vaccine. At the University of Michigan in Ann Arbor, Francis compiled a 113-page report. Less than half of one percent (0.4 percent) of the children inoculated experienced minor reactions.[1] Of the 1,829,916 children, 1,013 cases of contracting wild polio were reported. Of these 1,013 cases, most were children in the control groups—either those who received the placebo or those where were merely observed—but not all.[2] For this reason, the vaccine was not deemed 100 percent effective. Francis also reported on the budget. The NFIP had spent approximately $7.5 million for the field trials and the evaluation.[3]

Francis planned to announce these findings at an NFIP meeting held on April 12, 1955. Francis sent invitations to more than 500 distinguished scientists, doctors, and medical researchers.[4]

That morning, the attendees filed into Rackham Lecture Hall at the University of Michigan. Reporters

Members of the media gather as Salk, *left*, Francis, *center*, and NFIP president Basil O'Connor, *right*, announce their polio vaccine findings at the NFIP meeting on April 12, 1955.

had come from around the country to document the event. One of the drug companies that had helped produce the vaccine sponsored a closed-circuit broadcast of the meeting, and television crews set up in back of the lecture hall and outside of the room. Fifty-four thousand doctors and medical researchers prepared to watch the meeting on television.[5]

The Announcement

At 10:00 a.m., Francis took the podium. Salk's teacher, mentor, boss, and adviser spoke for an hour and a half, explaining every detail of the polio field trial. He predicted the vaccine would be from 60 to 90 percent effective in preventing polio.[6] One sentence from his speech especially stood out: "The vaccine works. It is safe, effective, and potent."[7]

The audience responded with respectful silence. Seated in the audience was Salk's wife, who held her sons' hands and let tears roll down her cheeks. A few scientists from Salk's laboratory wept as well. Salk himself sat calmly in his seat. He knew the benefits and risks, and he already knew his vaccine worked. Inside and outside of the lecture hall, reporters grabbed telephones and called in their stories. They began breaking the news that the polio vaccine worked.

At noon, the president of the NFIP introduced Salk. The crowd rose to their feet in a standing ovation. At the podium, Salk waited until the applause died and the audience sat down. He spoke for 15 minutes. In his speech, Salk thanked Francis, the NFIP, the pharmaceutical companies, and all the children of the field trial. But he failed to thank his own staff, never once mentioning their names. They sat stunned and hurt in the audience.

STAFF SUPPORT—AND SLIGHTS

Eleven members of Salk's senior staff sat in the audience of the NFIP event on April 12, 1955. Some had worked with Salk since the beginning. Members of the staff who Salk forgot to thank and mention in his speech included: army major and lab technician Byron Bennett, who had worked with Salk earlier on influenza; Julius Youngner, a World War II veteran with a PhD in microbiology; and Elsie Ward, a zoologist who specialized in growing viruses. Lorraine Friedman was Salk's administrative manager and was also present for the event.

As Salk thanked several groups of people during his speech—including millions of children who participated in the trials, but were strangers to him—members of his staff, many who had worked side-by-side with Salk for eight years, grew more and more upset. As Salk was bombarded by the media upon leaving Rackam Hall, the staff members slunk out unnoticed. One was so upset at being slighted that he cried openly on his subway ride home. Whether Salk made apologies for his misstep is unknown.

Salk left the stage. People pressed forward to speak to him. It took him an hour to move through the room. He found Donna and their three sons, and the family struggled to leave the building. On the way, they passed CBS journalist Edward R. Murrow. He told Salk, "Young man, a great tragedy has befallen you. You've lost your anonymity."[8]

Instant Fame

The news spread across the country. Stories printed in evening newspapers and the next morning. Salk's photograph appeared on front pages with triumphant headlines. "Salk Polio Vaccine Proves Successful," read one from the *New York Times*.[9] The Pittsburgh Press claimed, "Polio is Conquered."[10] The articles all delivered the same message: the Salk vaccine worked. It was safe, strong, and ready for use. Widespread vaccination would begin right away.

That evening, after the announcement, Salk appeared on a CBS television show called "See It Now." On the program, Salk once again spoke with journalist Murrow. At one point, Murrow asked, "Who owns the patent on this vaccine?" Salk replied, "Well, the people, I would say. There is no patent. Could you patent the

A representative of the people of Pittsburgh welcomes the Salks home with a bouquet of roses on April 16, four days after the polio vaccine announcement.

sun?"[11] It was a humane and selfless statement. President Dwight D. Eisenhower issued an equally humane executive order: Salk's vaccine would be freely given in the United States, and 75 countries worldwide could mass-produce it as well.[12]

Salk and his family stayed in Ann Arbor for four days. They posed for pictures, and Salk granted nonstop interviews for reporters. The Salks were eager to return to their quiet home life. When their flight landed in Pittsburgh, however, hundreds of citizens greeted them.

President Eisenhower honors Salk on April 22,
1955, for creating the polio vaccine.

The Salks needed a police escort to drive home. When they arrived home, they found a mountain of cards, letters, and telegrams piled at the front door, as well as gifts of flowers, food, and money. A Texas radio station had even bought Salk a new car. Salk was offered book and movie deals and was asked to collaborate making a line of clothing products. The fame from the vaccine reached its peak on April 22, 1955, when Salk and his wife stood in the White House Rose Garden as President Eisenhower himself thanked Salk for his service to the country.

The success of Salk's vaccine became a key moment in history. People united to celebrate the end of the 50-year reign of polio. Salk returned home to work in his lab. But his life would never return to the way it used to be. Reporter Murrow had been right. Salk was famous.

"Because of a signal and historic contribution to human welfare by Dr. Jonas E. Salk in his development of a vaccine to prevent paralytic poliomyelitis, I, Dwight D. Eisenhower, President of the United States, on behalf of the people of the United States, present to him this citation for his extraordinary achievement.

"The work of Dr. Salk is in the highest tradition of selfless and dedicated medical research. He has provided a means for the control of a dread disease."[13]

— An excerpt from a statement released by the White House on April 29, 1955, thanking Salk and the NFIP for their accomplishment

CHAPTER
EIGHT

LEAPS AND SETBACKS

U pon the conclusion of the trial, widespread vaccination began in the United States. On April 27, 1955, 15 days after the announcement, a vaccinated child got polio. Soon, other children contracted post-vaccine polio. In all cases, the paralysis began in the injected arm. It was determined that the shots had definitely caused the paralysis. This was Salk's worst nightmare, the very thing he had worked to prevent. Health officials responded quickly and tracked the polio cases. The infected children had all received a vaccine made by Cutter Laboratories in Berkeley, California. Cutter, in a rush to manufacture the drug, did not test all batches. Some of the lab's vaccine contained live poliovirus.

Salk grieved for the patients and their families. The general public once again had cause to fear polio. Children might get polio if they were not vaccinated.

After Salk's trial and announcement in April 1955, widespread production and delivery of his vaccine began across the country.

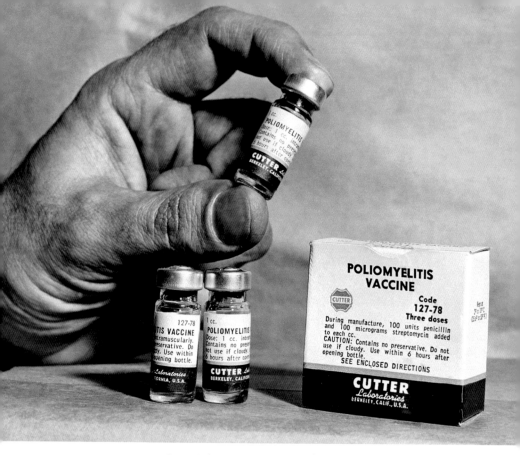

Cutter Laboratories' version of Salk's vaccine, April 1955

But they might get polio if they were vaccinated. US
Surgeon General Leonard Scheele called medical
scientists to an emergency meeting. He did not consult
Salk, in case blame lay with his techniques. It was
determined that only Cutter's vaccine caused problems.
Still, some scientists voted to halt the entire polio
vaccination program. Some blamed Salk for the disaster.
On April 27, the surgeon general ordered Cutter
Laboratories to recall its vaccine. Taking no chances,
Scheele also temporarily halted all polio vaccinations,

ordering safety checks of every laboratory that was producing Salk's vaccine.

On May 8, Scheele appeared on television and explained that the Public Health Service needed to check all drug companies making the polio vaccine. At the end of his talk, Scheele said, "We have every faith that this vaccine—the brilliant achievement of an able scientist, Dr. Jonas Salk, whose work has been so generously supported by the National Foundation for Infantile Paralysis—is both safe and effective. I believe that . . . within a few days, all of us will be able to move forward in the fight against polio with renewed confidence."[1]

On May 27, Scheele announced polio vaccinations could begin again. Salk was relieved. He said, "The margin of safety is now so clearly understood that only the grossest human error can upset it."[2]

The Cutter Case

The problem became known as "the Cutter Incident," and a case against Cutter Laboratories was brought to court. A jury determined the children's polio was indeed caused by the vaccine. But was the laboratory to blame? Some people pointed fingers at Salk, and he was asked to respond to the question of Cutter Laboratories'

CUTTER SKIPS SALK'S INSTRUCTIONS

When Salk released his vaccine to the public, he provided clear instructions on how to produce it. His instructions were similar to a recipe in which every step had to be followed exactly. These steps included applying the right amount of chemical to the virus, allowing the mix to sit at a precise temperature for an exact length of time, and conducting safety checks at every step. Salk studied Cutter Laboratories reports and saw the problem in their process. The corporation had omitted safety tests during one of the steps: the virus inactivation process.

negligence. In response, Salk wrote a 142-page report of his own findings. He revealed his vaccine was safe if prepared correctly, killing all the polio cells. Salk had produced countless batches of safe vaccine in his own laboratory. To mass-produce the vaccine, he stated, laboratories had to follow the proper steps. Salk did not criticize Cutter Laboratories outright, but his message was clear: Cutter Laboratories had failed. In the final count, at least 220,000 were infected with the live poliovirus from Cutter Laboratories' vaccine.[3]

Of these, 70,000 developed muscle weakness, 164 were severely paralyzed, and 10 died.[4] Some people who developed paralysis had received the vaccine, and others were family members or friends who were infected by the individual who received the shot.

As the case continued, Salk found himself in a web of politics. A Cutter lawyer brought in an expert from the University of California. Nobel Prize–winning virologist Wendell M. Stanley testified against Salk. Stanley accused Salk of using unsafe methods for mass production. His opinion was that Cutter Laboratories had followed government regulations and not broken any laws. After two days, the jury voted ten to two to acquit Cutter Laboratories, finding the corporation not guilty of negligence. Cutter Laboratories did have to pay damage charges to families hit by polio caused by the vaccine, however, and it was banned from making any more polio vaccine.

Salk realized he could not erase polio by himself. He made the vaccine, but he could not control its mass production. In one interview, he said, "All of the problems of man, all of the

SUCCESS AND CRITICISM

Despite Salk's successes, as society largely hailed him as a hero, controversy did surround his work. Salk was nominated for the Nobel Prize in 1955, 1956, 1958, and 1959 but never won the prize. He was also denied acceptance into the National Academy of Sciences. Sabin, on the other hand, was elected to the academy early in his career, in 1951. Some members of the medical science field criticized Salk, saying he did not discover anything new and that he used the work of others. Sabin once called Salk's work "kitchen chemistry."[5] Salk was also accused of being an attention seeker.

human problems if you like, will not be solved in the laboratory alone."[6]

A Switch

From 1955 to 1958, polio cases dropped dramatically in the United States. In 1959, polio spiked again. The number of cases rose to 8,425.[7] The reason for the spike was again traced to human error. The vaccine had to be given in three doses, one injection every two to three

LIVE VACCINE SUCCESS ABROAD

The entire time Salk had been creating his killed vaccine, Sabin was working on a live vaccine. In his lab at the University of Cincinnati, Sabin began his work with a strain of live poliovirus, weakening the cells just enough to trigger antibodies but not cause polio. Sabin believed his vaccine had many benefits over Salk's. Sabin made an oral vaccine that could be taken by mouth as a single dose, by placing two drops of the vaccine on a little bit of sugar. This inoculating procedure made Sabin's vaccination much simpler than Salk's. With Sabin's inoculation method, there was no need for a supply of needles, sterile equipment, and trained medical staff. This simpler immunization process was beneficial in countries that wanted to distribute the vaccine but did not have strong health-care systems.

Some countries had trouble producing Salk's vaccine. The Soviet Union was one example, and the country invited Sabin to test his live vaccine there. The Soviet government believed Sabin's vaccine would be easier to make and administer. Between 1958 and 1959, Sabin led a large clinical trial in Russia. He inoculated 13 million children with the live vaccine and effectively lowered cases of polio in Russia.[8]

weeks. Some families did not make sure their children got all three shots, perhaps thinking it was unnecessary. After a polio outbreak, however, people became convinced to follow the regimen. In 1961, the number of American children who contracted polio dropped to 1,312. After being in use for six years, the vaccine had brought down polio cases 98 percent from what they had been nine years earlier.[9]

As Salk's vaccine found success and began widespread distribution, Sabin, who had also received funding to research and develop his live polio vaccine, also began promoting his work. Everyone, including Salk, was surprised when the US government made a switch. The Sabin vaccines were licensed for use in 1961 and 1962, and the US government began using Sabin's live vaccine over Salk's killed vaccine. Sabin's vaccine was cheaper and easier to dispense. Doctors could drop the required dose onto a sugar cube and pop it into a child's mouth. By 1963, virtually all vaccinations for polio in the United States used the Sabin vaccine. After the switch to this vaccine, cases of polio in the United States dropped to record lows. In 1969, there were only 20 cases reported in the United States.[10]

Although Salk and Sabin disagreed with each other over science, their morals were in sync. Just as Salk had not patented his vaccine, Sabin also had not. Neither desired to profit from the vaccines but instead simply wanted to make safe vaccines available for everyone.

Although polio cases dropped significantly with Sabin's vaccine, the debate whether the living or the killed polio vaccine was better was not over. Sabin's living vaccine had caused isolated cases of polio. In those severe cases, the living vaccine changed back into the full poliovirus. The vaccine also mutated to a dangerous form and released a potent virus into the environment. Not only were vaccinated children infected but they more easily spread the disease to people around them. The newer form of the disease even got its own name: vaccine-associated paralytic poliomyelitis, or VAPP. The problems VAPP created would not be addressed for many decades.

The debate over which vaccine was superior—the live vaccine Sabin, *left*, created or the killed virus vaccine Salk, *right*, created—continued for many years.

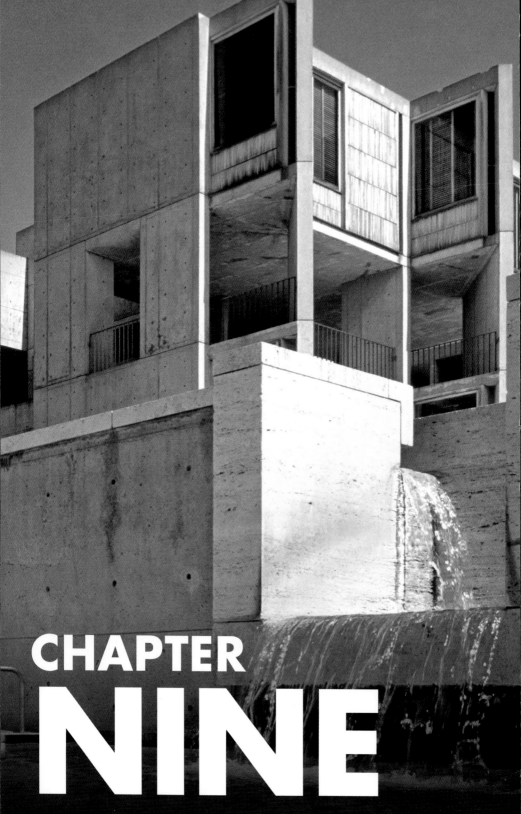

CHAPTER
NINE

BUILDING A DREAM

During much of Salk's career, basement laboratories were standard. Salk spent a lot of time in them himself, but he grew tired of the setting. He wanted to build a place where people could do "scientific work in a work of art."[1] Salk had long envisioned a place where scientists could work together on goals important to humanity. He said,

> I thought that it would be well to consider establishing an institution that would be concerned not merely with nature, but with the human side of nature, not only with the molecular, cellular dimension, but what I call the human dimension.[2]

In 1960, Salk worked with architect Louis Kahn on a modern concrete design that would bring his vision to life. The buildings would overlook the Pacific Ocean on land donated by the city of San Diego, California. It was important to Salk that the buildings be architecturally stunning. He felt the physical differences of the building would bring changes into the medical community.

The Salk Institute for Biological Studies in La Jolla, California

In 1963, with financial support from the NFIP, the Salk Institute for Biological Studies opened in La Jolla, California.

In the years following the opening of Salk's institute, his life continued changing rapidly. His oldest son, Peter, graduated from Harvard University in 1965. Following in his father's footsteps, Peter went on to study medicine, enrolling at Johns Hopkins University School of Medicine. While Peter was in medical school, in 1967, Salk and his wife decided to divorce. Newly single, with grown-up children, Salk began a new chapter in his life.

A New Start

In La Jolla in the summer of 1969, Salk's friends introduced him to the French artist Françoise Gilot. Salk invited Gilot on a tour of his institute. Although the two came from different worlds, science and art, they talked and found common ground in their work. Art and science, after all, both involve experimentation and trial and error.

In 1970, Salk and Gilot married in a small, private ceremony near Paris, France, which is where Gilot's mother lived. The couple returned to California

Françoise Gilot and Salk after their civil wedding ceremony in Paris

and moved into a house with a view of the Pacific
Ocean. Gilot's influence strengthened Salk's interest
in art. "Jonas has always been interested in art and
architecture," Gilot told a reporter. "He has curiosity
in many fields, not just science."[3] During his years with
Gilot, Salk explored painting, poetry, and philosophy.

He wrote his first books, *Man Unfolding*, in 1972, and *The Survival of the Wisest*, in 1973. Over the years, Salk and Gilot also traveled many places around the world, including Greece and Italy.

Honors

For several decades following his vaccination achievement, Salk continued to be granted recognition and honors. These honors include the Mellon Institute Award, a United States Presidential Citation, and a Congressional Gold Medal. He was also awarded honorary degrees from universities in the United States, Great Britain, Israel, Italy, and the Philippines. In 1976, Salk was inducted into the Academy of Achievement.

FRANÇOISE GILOT

In a 1979 article in *People* magazine, Salk reflected on his marriage to Françoise Gilot. "She is very logical and more pragmatic than I," he said. "Sometimes I get wrapped up in details, but she attacks things and dissects them straight on. I could have been an artist and she could have been a scientist."[4]

In 1993, to honor the thirtieth anniversary of his institute, Salk hung one of Gilot's paintings in the building. The painting had a scientific bent. "It's interesting," he said, "to see how she has incorporated the double helix and structures of fourteen molecules in this marvelous work of art."[5]

On July 11, 1977, President Jimmy Carter presented Salk with the Medal of Freedom in Washington, DC.

During these years, Salk always returned to his scientific work. He also began exploring his interest in human knowledge and wisdom. He studied behaviors and the way people make decisions. Salk was interested in learning how society makes collective decisions, especially ones that determine the future. In 1990, Salk said in an interview, "I have come to recognize evolution not only as an active process that I am experiencing all the time but as something I can guide by the choices I make, by the experiments I design."[6]

At his institute, Salk also focused his attention on the autoimmune disease HIV/AIDS. He began working with his son Peter in 1991. Together, they attempted to develop a vaccine to prevent HIV, the virus that leads to AIDS. They also searched for a way to prevent people with HIV from getting AIDS.

As Salk looked back on his career, he saw that his choices led him to be in the right place at the right time

> "He was an [eternal] optimist. He always believed that good things would prevail, especially if one worked hard for them."[7]
> —Salk's son, Dr. Darrell Salk

to study polio: studying science instead of law, becoming a medical researcher instead of a physician, and taking the job at the University of Pittsburgh. It seemed every decision led to his work with polio. Salk applied the same principles of medical research to his own life. If something does not go right, try again. Do something else. Go a different way. Ask more questions.

Salk died suddenly of heart failure on June 23, 1995, in La Jolla. He was 80 years old. Salk's legacy lives on, and work continues at the institute he founded. All three of his sons became physicians. Peter, the oldest, continues working on the projects related to HIV/AIDS he and his father worked on before Salk's death. Darrell works with biotechnology companies to develop new products. Jonathan is a psychiatrist who works with adolescent children.

Salk, at his institute in California, continued his passion for eradicating disease with vaccination throughout his life.

The medical world studied the two polio vaccines, Salk's killed and Sabin's live, for decades. In 2000, the Centers for Disease Control stated the Salk vaccine should once again be the main means of controlling polio in the United States. Today, the Salk vaccine is a standard part of the childhood vaccine regimen. People in the United States no longer worry about their children contracting polio. The virus is in a postvaccine stage and has almost disappeared. Near the end of Salk's life, he would every once in a while meet someone who had never heard of polio or Jonas Salk. His son Jonathan recalled this was the best compliment his father could receive.

TIMELINE

1914
Jonas Salk is born in New York City on October 28.

1929
Salk graduates from Townsend Harris High School at age 15 and enrolls in the City College of New York.

1938
The National Foundation for Infantile paralysis (NFIP), also known as the March of Dimes, is founded on January 3.

1939
Salk graduates from the New York University School of Medicine on June 8.

1939
Salk marries Donna Lindsay on June 9.

1942
Salk completes his medical internship at Mount Sinai Hospital.

1942

Salk accepts a job in the lab of Doctor Thomas Francis, head of the Department of Epidemiology at the University of Michigan.

1944

Salk's first son, Peter, is born.

1947

Salk's second son, Darrell, is born.

1947

Salk becomes director of the Virus Research Laboratory at the University of Pittsburgh School of Medicine.

1948

Salk begins work on the polio typing project.

1950

Salk's third son, Jonathan, is born.

1951

The NFIP approves and will fund Salk's pursuit of a polio vaccine.

TIMELINE

1953
Salk delivers a radio address called "The Scientist Speaks for Himself" on March 26.

1954
A trial of Salk's polio vaccine begins, with nearly 2 million children participating. It is the largest field trial in US history.

1955
On April 12, Salk and Francis announce the polio vaccine is ready for widespread distribution.

1955
The Cutter Laboratories incident halts polio vaccination from April 27 to May 27.

1961
After six years of use, Salk's vaccine has reduced polio cases 98 percent.

1962

In the United States, Sabin's live vaccine replaces Salk's killed vaccine.

1963

The Salk Institute for Biological Studies opens in La Jolla, California.

1970

Salk marries French painter Françoise Gilot.

1995

On June 23, Salk dies in La Jolla at age 80.

2000

Salk's killed vaccine once again becomes the standard method of polio immunization in the United States.

2005

A celebration of the fiftieth anniversary of the announcement of the Salk vaccine is held at the University of Pittsburgh on April 12. Another celebration is held in Rackham Hall on the University of Michigan campus.

ESSENTIAL FACTS

Date of Birth
October 28, 1914

Place of Birth
New York City, New York

Date of Death
June 23, 1995

Parents
Daniel and Dora Salk

Education
Townsend Harris High School
The City College of New York
New York University School of Medicine

Marriage
Donna Lindsay (June 9, 1939–1967)
Françoise Gilot (June 29, 1970–June 23, 1995)

Children
Peter, Darrell, and Jonathan

Career Highlights
Salk accepted a job as director of the virus laboratory at the University of Pittsburgh in 1947 and began creating the polio vaccine.

In 1954, 1.8 million children, called Polio Pioneers, were involved in a field trial of Salk's vaccine. It was the largest field test in medical history. Salk declared the polio vaccine ready for widespread use on April 12, 1955.

The Salk Institute for Biological Studies opened in 1963.

Societal Contribution

Salk created a safe and effective polio vaccine using inactivated, or killed, poliovirus. It helped virtually wipe out the disease in the United States and in many places worldwide. Later in life, Salk built a research institute and began studying HIV/AIDS, with his work aiding continued research on the disease.

Conflicts

Salk created a killed vaccine to prevent polio, which was considered impossible by leading scientists at the time. These scientists believed only living vaccines, containing the active virus, could prevent viruses. Albert Sabin was Salk's biggest opponent. Sabin created the living polio vaccine, which, for a time, became the primary polio vaccine over Salk's killed version. In recent years, however, Salk's vaccine has once again become the vaccine of choice in the United States.

Quote

"Risks, I like to say, always pay off. You learn what to do or what not to do."—*Jonas Salk*

GLOSSARY

antibody
A protein produced by the immune system to neutralize foreign cells, such as bacteria or viruses.

attenuated
Weakened or reduced in force.

epidemiology
The study of health and diseases.

immune
Protected from an illness.

immunization
The process of protecting the body against disease by vaccinating.

inoculate
To expose a person to a vaccine to build immunity.

iron lung

An artificial respirator that applies periodic pressure on the chest wall to force air in and out of the lungs.

placebo

A substance that is void of medicine, given to compare the results of those who received the medicine against those who did not.

quarantine

A restraint upon the activities of persons or the transport of goods to prevent the spread of disease.

virology

The branch of medicine that studies viruses and viral diseases.

virus

A small, infectious agent that grows only inside the living cells of humans, animals, and plants.

ADDITIONAL RESOURCES

Selected Bibliography

"Jonas Salk, M.D.: Jonas Salk Interview, Developer of Polio Vaccine." *Academy of Achievement*. American Academy of Achievement, 16 May 1991. Web. 9 Apr. 2013.

Kluger, Jeffrey. *Splendid Solution: Jonas Salk and the Conquest of Polio*. New York: Putnam, 2004. Print.

Oshinsky, David M. *Polio: An American Story*. New York: Oxford UP, 2005. Print.

Further Readings

Kehret, Peg. *Small Steps: The Year I Got Polio*. 2nd edition. Morton Grove, IL: Albert Whitman, 2006. Print.

Peters, Stephanie True. *The Battle Against Polio*. (Epidemic!) New York: Benchmark, 2005. Print.

Wilson, Daniel J. *Polio*. Santa Barbara, CA: Greenwood, 2009. Print.

Web Sites

To learn more about Jonas Salk, visit ABDO Publishing Company online at **www.abdopublishing.com.** Web sites about Jonas Salk are featured on our Book Links page. These links are routinely monitored and updated to provide the most current information available.

Places to Visit

Department of Biological Sciences, University of Pittsburgh

4249 Fifth Avenue
Pittsburgh, PA 15260
412-624-8286
http://www.biology.pitt.edu
The Department of Biological Sciences serves undergraduate and graduate students. The K-12 Outreach program shares its science resources with teachers and students in the community.

The Museum of Science and Industry

5700 S. Lake Shore Drive
Chicago, IL 60637
773-684-1414
http://www.msichicago.org
This museum has many science exhibits, including some on medical technology. Visitors to the YOU! Laboratory can see what it is like to attend medical school and treat a patient.

Salk Institute for Biological Studies

10010 North Torrey Pines Road
La Jolla, CA 92037
858-453-4100
http://www.salk.edu
The Salk Institute, designed by Jonas Salk and architect Louis Kahn, offers guided architectural tours.

SOURCE NOTES

Chapter 1. On the Verge of a Breakthrough

1. Jeffrey Kluger. *Splendid Solution: Jonas Salk and the Conquest of Polio*. New York: Putnam, 2004. Print. 189.

2. "History." *PolioToday.org*. Salk Institute for Biological Studies, 2013. Web. 22 Apr. 2013.

3. "Section I: Poliomyelitis, Treatment, and Prevention Prior to 1955: C. Epidemic Emergence (1880–1920)." *VaccineEthics.org*. Greenwall Foundation, n.d. Web. 22 Apr. 2013.

4. David M. Oshinsky. *Polio: An American Story*. New York: Oxford UP, 2005. Print. 11.

5. "What Ever Happened to Polio?: Communities." *National Museum of American History*. Smithsonian Institution, n. d. Web. 22 Apr. 2013.

6. Jeffrey Kluger. *Splendid Solution: Jonas Salk and the Conquest of Polio*. New York: Putnam, 2004. Print. 189.

7. "Jonas Salk, M.D.: Interview." *Academy of Achievement*. American Academy of Achievement, 16 May 1991. Web. 22 Apr. 2013.

Chapter 2. A Driven Student

1. "What Ever Happened to Polio?: Communities." *National Museum of American History*. Smithsonian Institution, n. d. Web. 22 Apr. 2013.

2. "The Pandemic." *The Great Pandemic: The United States in 1918–1919*. US Department of Health and Human Services, n. d. Web. 22 Apr. 2013.

3. Carol R. Byerly. "Public Health Reports: The US Military and the Influenza Pandemic of 1918–1919." *PubMed Central*. National Library of Medicine, National Institutes of Health, 2010. Web. 22 Apr. 2013.

4. "Jonas Salk, M.D.: Interview." *Academy of Achievement*. American Academy of Achievement, 16 May 1991. Web. 22 Apr. 2013.

5. Ibid.

Chapter 3. Medical School

1. "Jonas Salk, M.D.: Interview." *Academy of Achievement*. American Academy of Achievement, 16 May 1991. Web. 22 Apr. 2013.

2. David M. Oshinsky *Polio: An American Story*. New York: Oxford UP, 2005. Print. 99.

Chapter 4. Budding Virologist

1. "James Hiller: Electron Microscope." *Lemels On-MIT: Inventor of the Week*. Massachusetts Institute of Technology, May 2003. Web. 22 Apr. 2013.

2. Jeffrey Kluger. *Splendid Solution: Jonas Salk and the Conquest of Polio*. New York: Putnam, 2004. Print. 58–60.

3. "About Science & AAAS." *Science*. American Association for the Advancement of Science, 2013. Web. 22 Apr. 2013.

4. "Jonas Salk, M.D.: Interview." *Academy of Achievement*. American Academy of Achievement, 16 May 1991. Web. 22 Apr. 2013.

5. Jeffrey Kluger. *Splendid Solution: Jonas Salk and the Conquest of Polio*. New York: Putnam, 2004. Print. 63–64.

6. "In Science News." *The Science News-Letter* 45.20 (May 13, 1944): 313. *JSTOR*. Web. 26 Apr. 2013.

7. Jeffrey Kluger. *Splendid Solution: Jonas Salk and the Conquest of Polio*. New York: Putnam, 2004. Print. 71–73.

Chapter 5. A Lab of His Own

1. "Jonas Salk, M.D.: Interview." *Academy of Achievement*. American Academy of Achievement, 16 May 1991. Web. 22 Apr. 2013.

2. David M. Oshinsky. *Polio: An American Story*. New York: Oxford UP, 2005. Print. 120.

3 . Jeffrey Kluger. *Splendid Solution: Jonas Salk and the Conquest of Polio*. New York: Putnam, 2004. Print. 130.

4. David M. Oshinsky. *Polio: An American Story*. New York: Oxford UP, 2005. Print. 120.

5. Harry M. Marks. "The 1954 Salk Poliomyelitis Vaccine Field Trial." *John Hopkins Medicine: History of Medicine*. Johns Hopkins University, 16 Feb. 2008. Web. 22 Apr. 2013.

6. "Jonas Salk, M.D.: Interview." *Academy of Achievement*. American Academy of Achievement, 16 May 1991. Web. 22 Apr. 2013.

Chapter 6. Testing the Vaccine

1. "John F. Enders: Nobel Lecture; The Cultivation of the Poliomyelitis Viruses in Tissue Culture." *Nobelprize.org*. Nobel Media, 2013. Web. 22 Apr. 2013.

2. Jeffrey Kluger. *Splendid Solution: Jonas Salk and the Conquest of Polio*. New York: Putnam, 2004. Print. 199.

3. "3/26/1953: Salk Becomes a Public Figure." *The History of Vaccines: Timelines*. College of Physicians of Philadelphia, 2013. Web. 22 Apr. 2013.

4. Jeffrey Kluger. *Splendid Solution: Jonas Salk and the Conquest of Polio*. New York: Putnam, 2004. Print. 220–221.

SOURCE NOTES CONTINUED

5. Anita Srikameswaran. "Finding the Polio Pioneers." *Post-Gazette.com*. PG Publishing, 19 Aug. 2003. Web. 22 Apr. 2013.

6. Richard Carter. *Breakthrough: The Saga of Jonas Salk*. New York: Trident, 1966. Print. 163.

7. "Jonas Salk, M.D.: Interview." *Academy of Achievement*. American Academy of Achievement, 16 May 1991. Web. 22 Apr. 2013.

8. Harry M. Marks. "The 1954 Salk Poliomyelitis Vaccine Field Trial." *John Hopkins Medicine: History of Medicine*. Johns Hopkins University, 16 Feb. 2008. Web. 22 Apr. 2013.

9. Jeffrey Kluger. *Splendid Solution: Jonas Salk and the Conquest of Polio*. New York: Putnam, 2004. Print. 234.

10. Ibid. 248–249.

11. Ibid. 254–255.

12. "On This Day: Lasting Prevention of Polio Reported in Vaccine Tests." *New York Times Learning Network*. New York Times, 2010. Web. 22 Apr. 2013.

Chapter 7. Breaking News

1. "1955 Polio Vaccine Trial Announcement." *University of Michigan School of Public Health*. University of Michigan, 5 June 2012. Web. 22 Apr. 2013.

2. Ibid.

3. Ibid.

4. Jeffrey Kluger. *Splendid Solution: Jonas Salk and the Conquest of Polio*. New York: Putnam, 2004. Print. 287–288.

5. Ibid.

6. Ibid. 294.

7. Ibid.

8. Ibid. 299.

9. Ibid. 301.

10. Ibid.

11. David M. Oshinsky. *Polio: An American Story*. Oxford University Press. 2005. Print. 211.

12. Jeffrey Kluger. *Splendid Solution: Jonas Salk and the Conquest of Polio*. New York: Putnam, 2004. Print. 302.

13. "Jonas Salk and the Polio Vaccine." *Dwight D. Eisenhower Presidential Library & Museum*. National Archives and Records Administration, 22 Apr. 1955. Web. 25 Apr. 2013.

Chapter 8. Leaps and Setbacks

1. Richard Carter. *Breakthrough: The Saga of Jonas Salk*. New York: Trident, 1966. Print. 325.

2. Ibid. 331.

3. Paul A. Offit. The Cutter Incident: *How America's First Polio Vaccine Led to the Growing Vaccine Crisis*. New Haven, CT: Yale UP, 2005. Print. 89.

4. Ibid.

5. Harold M. Schmeck Jr. "On This Day: June 24, 1995: Dr. Jonas Salk, Whose Vaccine Turned Tide on Polio, Dies at 80." *New York Times Learning Network*. New York Times, 24 June 1995. Web. 22 Apr. 2013.

6. "Open Mind: Interview with Jonas Salk." *YouTube*. YouTube, 7 June 2011. Web. 22 Apr. 2013.

7. Jeffrey Kluger. "Conquering Polio." *Smithsonian.com*. Smithsonian Institution, Apr. 2005. Web. 22 Apr. 2013.

8. Jeffrey Kluger. *Splendid Solution: Jonas Salk and the Conquest of Polio*. New York: Putnam, 2004. Print. 316.

9. Ibid. 314.

10. Ibid. 317.

Chapter 9. Building a Dream

1. "Jonas Salk, M.D.: Interview." *Academy of Achievement*. American Academy of Achievement, 16 May 1991. Web. 22 Apr. 2013.

2. Ibid.

3. Suzy Kalter. "At 57, Francoise Gilot Recalls Life with Picasso but Enjoys It with Scientist Jonas Salk." *People*. Time, 30 July 1979. Web. 22 Apr. 2013.

4. Ibid.

5. "Jonas Salk, M.D.: Interview." *Academy of Achievement*. American Academy of Achievement, 16 May 1991. Web. 22 Apr. 2013.

6. Harold M. Schmeck Jr. "On This Day: June 24, 1995: Dr. Jonas Salk, Whose Vaccine Turned Tide on Polio, Dies at 80." *New York Times Learning Network*. New York Times, 24 June 1995. Web. 22 Apr. 2013.

7. "Selected Questions from Student Interviews: Darrell Salk, M.D." *The Jonas Salk Center*. Darrell Salk, 2001. Web. 22 Apr. 2013.

INDEX

ABOUT THE AUTHOR

Sheila Llanas lives in Milwaukee, Wisconsin. She taught writing at the Johns Hopkins Center for Talented Youth (CTY) and the University of Wisconsin–Waukesha for seven years each. She has written more than 30 informational books for young readers.

ABOUT THE CONSULTANT

Daniel J. Wilson has been a professor of history at Muhlenberg College since 1978. His scholarly training focused on the intellectual and cultural history of the United States, which included the history of medicine and public health, as well as epidemics that affected the nation. While Wilson has studied and taught a wide breadth of US history topics during his career, since the 1990s, he has focused his scholarly work on the history of US polio epidemics. Wilson's expertise centers specifically on polio epidemics that occurred in the United States prior to Salk's 1955 vaccine. He has written three books and published numerous articles on these epidemics.